KUDZU
SELECTED POEMS

By the same author:
Trio in a Mirror
(*University of Arizona Press*, 1960)
Houses (*Burning Deck*, 1970)

DOROTHY DONNELLY
# KUDZU
## AND OTHER POEMS
### NEW AND SELECTED
POURBOIRE PRESS
1978

Some of these poems were first published in the following magazines: *Arbor, Burning Deck, Christian Century, Commonweal, Counter/Measures, Critic, Hudson Review, Ladies Home Journal, Michigan Quarterly, Modern Poetry Studies, National Catholic Reporter, National Review, New Yorker, Poetry, Spectrum.*

This project has been supported by a grant from the National Endowment for the Arts in Washington, D.C., a federal agency.

Copyright © 1978 by Dorothy Donnelly.

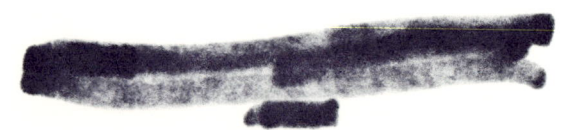

CONTENTS

Kudzu   1
A Prospect of Swans   3
Glass World   5
Blue Flag   6
The Venus of Willendorf   8
The Pink Mite   9
Large View from a Small Window   10
Violets   11
The Magic Dimension   12
Hollyhock   13
A Small Thing   14
Two Figures in a Golden Light   15
Spiderwork I   16
Spiderwork II   17
To Three Old Ladies   18
Leaflight   20
Figurine   21
A Rose is a Rose   22
The Point of a Pin   23
Dandelions   24
As Far as the Eye Can Reach   25
To Begin With   27
Suns and Straws   28
A Toast Long Overdue   29
The Earthworm   31
Flowerfall   33
Roses of Ashes   34
Houses   35
R as in Garnet   42
Crayon Monster   43
Consider the Lilies   44
Sky Writing   45
Intimations of Mortality   46

*Selected Poems*
Swan     49
Three-Toed Sloth     50
Trio in a Mirror     52
Afternoon of a Gnat     59
A Concern for Beauty     60
Chinese Baby Asleep     62
Spider Compared to Star     63
Charm     66
Cardinal's Chick     67
Postcard: Bones of a Sabre-Tooth Tiger     68
Serenade     70
Alexandrina     71
Snowflakes     73
For Peter Who Cried Because He Could Not Catch the Moth     74
Wheels     75
Wild Plums at Pha-An     77
Perennial Landscape     78
Skyblue Monday     79
Girandole     81
People     82

# KUDZU
SELECTED POEMS

KUDZU

That famed and feigning genie
who rose up out of the vase
   the fisherman found,
   and swelled from a wisp
to a massive monster of mist
   that reached the clouds
and covered half a sea

has a real rival in the kudzu
which pulls itself out of itself
   like bushels of silk
   from a hat, a vine
whose magic-beanstalk climb
   is as strange, though a fact,
as the fake rope-act of the Hindu.

From a pinpoint start it spreads
right up to the roof—on the scale
   of an ostrich hatched
   from an aphid's egg;
and though it hasn't a leg
   to stand on, it stands
twenty feet over our heads.

Equipped for competitive action,
this plant comes armed, is rough,
   all saw-teeth, prickles,
   and runners with rasps
for feet with which it grasps,
   gropes, and shoves
its way by serpentine traction.

It has, if balked of rising,
tricks up its sleeve: it will crawl,
  clutch at a straw,
  rear like a snake
scouting for prey, then strike,
  and curl in its coils
some Laocoön doomed to strangling.

But if those tentacle tendrils
find tall things to cling to, up
  go the leaves, high, wide,
  and as handsome as
the Corinthian acanthus,
  advancing two
by two, as alike as stencils.

Growing less, it grows more, begets
begetters. What genie could match it,
  this kudzu which conjures
  by natural acts
the hundreds of green acrobats
  waiting their turn
to climb, that pack its pockets?

## A PROSPECT OF SWANS

We came out through the high doors, our heads
full of Daumiers and Delacroix's, and still
elated, descended the marble steps;
and across the water a swan moved toward us,
noble, and slow as the slowest pavane.

As if she had a year and a day,
she delayed, as if she knew admirers
stood on the stair before her, that the rose
of the sunset opened behind her—alone,
illumined, afloat on an acre of lake.

And while we watched, approving the poise
and the pose, she suddenly dove, turned up-
side down like any goose, submerging
her head, like a moose after lily pads
or lily roots—a working bird

like others. Here was no opera swan,
nor emblematical, but animal,
her sinuous alabaster figure
proof enough that a thing of beauty
turns the eye, and will forever.

At an early age, with love at first sight,
seated on a hard, black, oval-backed chair
under a gas-globe light in a room
with more past than my own, I saw through the two
glass eyes of the stereopticon

my first swan, on a pond under ostrich-
tail palms, molded, so it seemed, of porcelain
or snow. That was long ago. I still
see swans, not dreamed-up like Sinbad's roc
but real as wrens. The swan is *not*

an ivory-tower type—the poets'
pet—but a bird preferred by the people.
She is everywhere: in Plato's prose,
adrift on the Avon, wan in watermarks,
flashing in neon. Though symbolists

and kings have claimed her, she refuses
to be exclusive, to be looked at only
by some presumptive royal eye,
but is visible to any idler or boy,
saunterer in parks, or gazer at the zoo.

Any day, soundless, gliding as on glass,
she may come into view on some lagoon
the green of celadon, framed
in the willow's fronds, clothed like the curved
camellia, whiter than winter's moons.

## GLASS WORLD

The still scene scintillates;
sparks swarm over the brier;
bare bushes blaze. Ice
is setting the world on fire.

A touch of sun on the sleet
turns the teasel to crystal,
and glances stars off the glass
stalks of the burdock and thistle.

On enamels of blue, a tree,
kindled by cold, air, and water,
lights up like a chandelier
in a flash of opals and umber.

*For Denis and Jackie*

## BLUE FLAG

Blue as the blowpipe's petal of flame,
the flag, afloat at the crest of the wave
of its leaves, unfurls an ephemeral crown,
three-tiered, nine-rayed, and girdled with jade.

Sealed, to begin with, in tissue, and stuck
to the stem in a curve like a locust's wing,
it rides into light in this envelope lean
as a leaf, too thin to hold a thing,

it would seem, till it opens and shows a ship-
in-a-bottle surprise: slim as a moth
at birth stands an elegant spindle, sea-purple
and patched with gold, that turns, no sloth

so slow, to a lily of chiseled gauze.
In curves as sharp as if carved with scalpels
from paper-thin slices of stone, inked in,
pen-fine, with damson lines like the marble's

veins, it spreads its spurs. It shows
its colors in yellow carpets plumed
with plush for the feet of the bee as she feels
her way over azure bridges and perfumed

paths, through tunnels down to the well-hid
wells where the diamond drop of nectar
is. All this to bring, spring
after spring, the seed to the bud to the flower

to the bee, again, again, and again
with undiminished esprit, to bear,
once more, the same lambent form as before,
afloat on its jewel-blue wings in the air.

## THE VENUS OF WILLENDORF

Not wafted onto a scene full of sun in a seafoam
shell by a Botticellian breeze, but dredged
from the dark, this caveman's Venus comes and startles us
into staring. Here is stone with a blown-glass bauble's
bubble outline, a form all orbs, clustered
like plums on a stem, a harmony of spheres, like them.

No stone-age code or cold convention but only
the boldness of love could account for that finial sphere,
that head as big as a sun, embellished with sculptured
scallops of hair; a cosmos encircled with curls
like a Saturn with rings. She has hips Lachaise would praise.
This anonymous nude, neither Parisian nor Greek,

was, in her own day, chic. Though nothing like Whistler's
"Mother" or Madame Recamier in a cloud
of tulle, on a sofa, sky-blue with a gilt swan's neck
for arm, she, too, has basked in an artist's eye;
she resembles, a little, some globe-headed lady by Klee
or one of those gourdshaped girls by Pablo Picasso.

Now, unearthed unharmed after twenty-five thousands
of years underground, this Venus with the beehive hair
is back in the eye of the world, plump as a mango,
shy as a bushful of birds. Adorned with bangles
and cosmetic reds, her egglike figure ends up
in its irreplaceable place in the landscape of love.

# THE PINK MITE

Science abhors a fiction, its forte being fact.
For facts it will fly to the moon (a feat once restricted
to fiction): it will move a mountain to prove a mouse.
Its game, as old as man, is questions-and-answers—
"How far down the globe do signs of life, extinct
or extant, extend? Are there tracks of its trek to the end?"

With the zeal of merchants searching for peerless pearls,
scientists, searching for answers, pushed toward the perilous
Pole on the heels of life, and past the last penguin,
in a world of cold, they found it, warming the heart
of a mite—a pinpoint of pink of whose ilk a herd
could have bivouacked beneath a snowflake. But size aside,

it was just as alive as a lion, and as much at home
on the adamant ice as a crocodile in plush mud
on the Nile. Survivor of terrible airs, it proved
how far life will go to plant its seeds, hatching
at the planet's frigidest inch an infinitesimal,
pink, pedestrian mite with a liking for lichen.

And when, unattended, the infant steps from the snug
egg, with its eight bare feet and small bald head,
is it cold? When it opens wide its mouth to be filled
in this wilderness, is it foiled? Oh, it does not want!
Led like the flock to grass, the pink mite feeds
in polar pastures, replete as a sheep on the green.

> "Pink Mite Discovered Near the South Pole
> —closer to the Pole than animal life has
> been known to exist...a hundredth of an
> inch long...found by a team of
> scientists..." Special to *The New York
> Times.*

## LARGE VIEW FROM A SMALL WINDOW

Outside the window, night
unmasks a sky as ornate
as a peacock, sprinkled with sparkles
that turn in the dark into marvels
of star-footed beasts and giants
with jeweled eyes. Orion
is rising conspicuously
with his lucid sword, three
double stars in his belt, and Rigel—
the titan spur in his heel—
seventeen thousand times
as bright as the sun that shines
on our own world. And aflash
and aglitter, the great gold Fish,
the Bull, the Lions, and the Dog
with blue Sirius held like an egg
in its mouth, shine out. And the Pleiades
glimmer with a light that leaps,
unimpeded, toward us for more
than three hundred years before
we see it, coming like mist
through cobweb out of a lost
colossus of two thousand stars
never seen! They are so far apart
that our sun and its satellite orbs
could roll between them like marbles,
so far off they are dwarfed in our sky
to a pale rosette on the red-eyed
Bull. But deep in the dark
abysses, that dazzle of stars
swarms over space in a horn
like a blown morning-glory's, of glory.

## VIOLETS

Like a conjurer shaking out doves
from his sleeves, spring comes and fills
the air with "inchanted trifles"—

with the robins' and the treefrogs' trills,
the frilled trilliums, and the violets'
sapphire perfume-flasks

unstoppered and rifled by the roving
bees that appear each year
when the buds, breaking open their seals,

release the packed-in petals
and the scents that lure the lovers
of nectar to the violets' phials.

## THE MAGIC DIMENSION

At two, like a putto stepped from a painting,
you stood surveying your waiting world,
a fillip of fun in your eyes, eager
as a bee flying toward a field of flowers,

to dive into the day. Once the trick of talk
(like walking a tightrope to learn) had come
to the tip of your tongue, your world was as changed
as a bird's when it first feels the air under

its feet. As eager for answers as a robin
for worms, you would ask whether sea-anemones
ever slept, or what squids did. Words
took you farther and faster than a flying carpet,

moved you into a magic dimension.
Then you could *say* what you *saw!* Like Copernicus
telling the world it ran circles around
the sun, you could tell your wonders to others,

and to you every bird and bug was new,
each with a name to be found out and called by
as you ran, keeping up with the day, under skies
pellucidly blue at untarnished two!

HOLLYHOCK

When it's time by summer's clock, the locked-in
hollyhock-bud breaks out of its jewel-case-
cage like a moth from an outgrown cocoon.

Ready at a signal to move, it waits
its turn on the stem where the buds open, one
above one, then uncurling its crumpled petals,

unfurls, forming a scallop-shell-flower
with a jade star in the heart of its garnet.
One after another, unfolding their fires,

the hollyhock-blossoms go up and up
the stiltlike stalk, till the last bell-flared
*belle fleur* perches, atilt, at the top.

## A SMALL THING

A small thing, glinting in the grass,
shone with an air, saying that,
like a painting or a bouquet,
it had been made to be looked at.

Some beginner, begun, like Braque
or Cezanne, with the gift to change
the familiar—green trees or grapes—
before one's eyes into strange

and enchanted shapes, had set
in the half of a clam shell, side
by side, three pale snails' coils,
a pink pebble, and five

mauve violets—nine
trifles trebled in color,
jeweled with the glow of the pooled
light lent one to the other.

Last in the picture, migrant,
mercurial, topping the tip
of a petal—so quick its feelers
and hair-fine feet, they split

the light like tinsel—a mite
with mica wings landed,
arrived like the rhinestone dew,
sparkling and unexpected.

## TWO FIGURES IN A GOLDEN LIGHT

This quaint Crivelli Christ-child curving toward you
out of the alcove of his mother's arm,
with his baby-Hercules leg and ballet-dancer's
sandaled foot, gold-fur curls, and rings
under his eyes, is not what one would expect;
nor could one beforehand imagine this Virgin, in vogue
in a velvet cloak with fleur-de-lys, gilt on green,
a fillet of pearls, and copper hair; for here
is the rise and "touch of strangeness," the surprise,
the unwonted and wanted that art is famous for.

Genius has breathed its metamorphoses
and a world emerged, like a genie's conjured fruit,
where things opaque and local take on fire like
the opal: a perse and marble earth beneath
a sky of brass where a burnished pear and an apple
rare as Atalanta's hang like planets,
pale beside the candent core, the heat
of the heart, the double love that turns these heads
to suns, their wreaths of radiance reaching across
the scarlet carpet stretched between them and us.

A world of art, apart, yet apparently
a world in which we have a part, this portrait
was made to make us, happily, look. See
how the golden faces gaze on us in a way
we like: the lady smiles with her topaz eyes,
and her long hand draws us into the picture,
while the Child's, upright like a flower afloat in light,
tells its urgent message, secret to each,
to everyone, saying fondly, "It is true,
the apple of my constant eye is *you!*"

## SPIDERWORK I

At dusk only a blur of blue air
fills the gap in the hedge, but at dawn
a delicate netting hangs there, diamonds
dangling from its flickering mesh. Fashioned

of water and silk, this baroque mobile
floating its jewels on space is the work
of the weaver-of-webs and the weather, together.
First, walking on air, the geometer-

spider unspools a thread from her black
sac and begins to spin, composing
with spiral and spoke the cells of the rose
window she's building for the gilded fly.

In the cool of the night the bright buds
of the dew break through the dark like cupids'
heads through painted sky, and every
ring of the wreath is rhinestone-rimmed

and dancing. Crowded with twinkling crystals
at dawn, by noon the silken trellis
is bare, those undurable diamonds gone
without trace into the pale turquoise air.

## SPIDERWORK II

Standing like an Andean Indian scanning
the chasm he plans to span, the spider
spots among plots of unoccupied space
a site that suits her. At once she unwinds

a hairfine line, then, feat of foot
as a goat, crosses the gap on that floating
cable, spinning, as she goes, silk spokes
and a spiral. Snare and delusion, the tricks

of the trapper, prosper the spider, a true
illusionist, using, guilelessly, ruses
that delude. Even the fly with its "thousands
of tiny six-sided eyes" can't elude

her weir of air-colored ropes that rope
the air. Though with no such intent, the orb-weaver
ornaments unadorned corners of space
with an openwork lace that turns, with the sun

on the dew, to a pearled-and-rubied rose window—
a view she is blind to. Appetite's the muse
that moves her, without knowing how or why,
to ply the antique art she lives by,

as, suspending her seine of invisible silk
in the sea of the air, she traps the passing
gnat—the unwitting cause of that filigree
flower of her labor, the net's rosette.

TO THREE OLD LADIES

Two old ladies, lured
  by the velvet night, leave
    the lee of their porch and go,

for a change of scene, abroad,
  a block from home. They wade
    through shadows past the black

catalpa's cataract
  to the corner, their ultima Thule,
    where clear of the cliffs of leaf

and the tall waterfall elm,
  they sight the sky and, in it,
    in perfect view a quarter

million miles from the eye,
  a face more famous than Helen's—
    worth a walk in the dark, to see

that lily-stately and ancient
  queen, dazzling in astral
    white, throned in the heavens,

reigning over the night.
  The travelers stare, unaware
    that the silver light which comes

so fast from so far has fallen
   onto their hair and sprinkled
      their hands with spangles. They linger,

like talkative tourists in front of
   the Mona Lisa, to praise her.
      Eloquently, with the ardor

of competing ciceroni
   extolling a masterpiece,
      they show each other the moon.

LEAFLIGHT

The trees turn:
flower-yellow
on the willow,
red of the rose
on maple boughs;
the sumacs burn.

The leaves fall:
walnut, alder,
poplar, elder;
and elms unveil,
dropping gold foil
on field and wall.

## FIGURINE

*In Memoriam Peter Ruthven*

The matter is minor: eight inches of sculpture from China,
made of clay, mostly grey with fish-scale touches of color,
where a scholar, at his ease in the bent-knee posture
    of the East,
squints down at the squat speckled bird perched on his wrist
which he, as a pleasure of his leisure, is about to feed
with a bean like a half-moon held between finger and
    thumb.

Made solely to be seen, like the round-eyed owlet on an
    obol
or a swanshape carved in a hedge, and no more needed
than gilt on a leaf's edge, this man-bird-and-bean bagatelle,
one of those "objects of virtu" such as the four-inch ivory
gazelle dug up in Thebes, diverts us; its only
virtue—its appeal—is its reward; when it pleases
    it succeeds.

This tomb figurine, whose aplomb holds the poise-loving eye
like a juggler's oranges whirling their suns round a hand-spun
sky or the flower-de-luce of a three-pronged fountain
in its balance of motion, possessed of that glow that outlasts
times and modes, lives on, as perennial in the affections
as an old Venetian glass nosegay, or an Aubosson rose.

## A ROSE IS A ROSE

Unraveling a rose for a clue
to its petaled poise, is to lose
the rose. Smashing an atom

to get to the x in its heart
bares another x in the heart
of each part. Pushing and shoving

won't faze poker-faced matter,
a tough partner to play with.
Flaying a flower to discover

the secret of its cinnabar skin
won't work—it can only unclothe,
it can never unriddle the rose.

# THE POINT OF A PIN

> *as seen under magnification "powerful enough to give a clear view of atoms of metals."*

Thus seen, what was seen before as a point
now appears as a pattern flowered from a thousand
scintillas of matter impeccably spaced
in kaleidoscope-spoked motifs as baroque

as the snowflakes' spiky shapes, ornate
to the tips of their tines. Affined from the first
to form, the amorphous dust becomes
crystals or chrysanthemums or these petaled

octets in the metal where lines concocted
of dots combine to compose designs
as symmetric as clocks. Now eyes, raised
to the nth power by the power of minds

over matter, can trace the medallions the little
particles make in the miniscule nets
of lace that lattice every least tittle
of space in the tin in the point of a pin.

For Robert Francis

## DANDELIONS

The dandelion, long expert in the arts
of survival, outmaneuvers numerous rivals
in the race for space by keeping the laws
it has no mind to change. A tapper
of wells, it can manage if the rainfall fails;

it can take, with its rough ruff of leaves, the lion's
share of the sun—while its neighbors take the shade.
When in want of outside aid, it baits
the go-between bee, coaxing her with syrup
from a gold, baroque cup. Not needing to run

(like the rat) or swim (like the swan) it has only
to stay where it is—in two places at once—
its foot in the ground (thus more than the earthworm
earthbound), its head high above, sharing
with the untethered moth, the unfettering air.

When its petals fall, an eiderdown dome
appears, a fairy-geometry sphere
ephemeral as foam, that goes when the wind blows.
Abetted by the breeze, it breaks into airy
parachute-fleets that deposit at random

the myriad gold-bearing seeds of next season's
crop of increased and multiplied, bold,
irrepressible weeds that the sun will tease
into pinwheels, awhirl like those firework stars
the artist saw from the café at Arles.

*In Memoriam Peter Kaplan*

## AS FAR AS THE EYE CAN REACH

The eye, bent on its own business,
pictures with camera art whatever
surface it sees—ruffle and ripple
of rose, reptile, river, or rock—
but stopped by the thinnest thatch, is blind
to a nested pearl a nail's breadth away,
unaware of fire and attar under
the veils and in the vials of matter.

Lapped, like the maize-ear in leaves, the earth
lies in its rind of suns and ring
of air and skin of oceans and dust,
rare wrappings that tease the Eve in us
to pierce to the heart of the puissant seed
that sent up the stalk that branched with herbs
and cattle and birds, and burgeoned into
the burning bush that the world is.

The quick seeds, kindling unseen,
keep the ultimate secret. Each
unfolds to its finish, fringed or gilded,
in fern or finch or fish not one
of which, though raveled and plucked like lovers'
daisies, piecemeal, yields a clue.
Eagle, apple—what lights their light
is dark. They issue out of a cloud,

luminaries that stream through earth,
water, and air on a scene where endlessly,
moons and violets rise, the swan
shines, dolphin and falcon flash
and glide, the tangerine burns among leaves.
Matter, mated with fire, buds
millionfold, the dark of its bush lighting up
as glowworms with gold, for the eye to see it by.

TO BEGIN WITH  "*the exquisite complexity of a smile...*"
 *Teilhard de Chardin*

To begin with, nobody smiles—but cries
begin with the first breath. Alarms
that sound at all hours, they're as apt at getting
help for the helpless as sirens or bells.

The little water-bug swirls that early
dimple the infant cheek, look like,
but aren't, the curves of smiles which only
slowly, as buds unfurl, unfold.

Not, like rain or the rainbow, formed
perforce, but framed on awakened delight,
the smile, in due time, dawns on the lips.
Transformed by its crescent, the face glows

and the eyes flash like new-lit candles
casting their beams—mites of light,
saying, in minim signs, that one more
immortal sun has begun to shine.

## SUNS AND STRAWS

Though the fall of an apple is not, like the fall
of a star, a spectacular act, *one* apple
rose, as it fell, to comet-fame
when Newton, noting it, saw in the flash
of its fall, the clue to the law of the fall

of all—straws and stones, oak trees
and sparrows and hairs. But earth, like a jealous
shepherd zealous for the sheep of his flock,
draws with her magni-magnet all matter's
scattered fragments back into her keep.

(Mysterious matter-mute, inscrutable,
dark indestructible stuff! Ever
at the beck of form, it will furnish flesh
for a flea or a flower; or fatten a worm;
or fur a tiger.) Not an atom is lost

from the plump planet's curvaceous figure.
Apple and apple-shaped earth, each
in its orbit, stand or fall by the laws
they're attuned to—a Pied Piper music that all
the spheres hear, that moves the millions of suns

through space and assembles the nebulas' clusters.
What Juggler, balancing galaxies like plates,
set those celestial corollas to spinning,
creating thereby a Versailles of lily-
bright lights and fountains across the sky!

## A TOAST LONG OVERDUE

To you, in front as usual,
always a little ahead of me,
always first, like a prow,
giving news as it comes into view
of the craft that lies behind it;
introducing me to the world,
the world to me;

speaking for, and sometimes well
(against my will) against me:
a not quite adequate advocate;
a confidential agent
to be watched—given to giving
what was meant to be kept; a hybrid—
half gossip, half sphinx.

To you, constant in change;
as swayed by passing moods
as tides by the moon; tempest-
tossed; the emotions' ocean;
a confirmed impressionist
true to a fault to the moment,
often false to me.

To you who nevertheless
look out for me, and even
in the teeth of the evidence act
in my best interests, fencing
in my defense, in weak
moments feinting for me;
in the end, my friend.

Mine to have and to hold,
for better, or more likely worse
the more time overtakes you;
I take you just as you are.
I drink to you—with your lips—
my life's companion, my own,
my only, face.

## THE EARTHWORM

The worm, on the move in his world, glides through clay
like a bird through air or a fish through the sea, only
more slowly. Though looked on as low for having little—
no head, no heart, not so much as a bone to his back—
he has, for his worm's role, all that is apropos.

Uninstructed, but not unskilled, he builds a house
after the plan of his clan by the blueprint in his blood.
He has tools: his torso (the perfect bore for his burrow)
and his tail (a trowel when he plasters his small front hall).
Unlike the monophagous moose which lives on leaves,

mostly, and roots, the worm, like omnivorous man,
devours fish, flesh, and flowers, putting them
into his mouth with his nose as the elephant does.
He chews like the toothless chicken; a few grains of grit
grinding inside him like millstones mince his meat.

Going his way, he gets himself into tight places
such as cracks in the mud; there he feels comforted—safe,
like the wearer of a bullet-proof vest. He protests attack
for though spineless he's laced with muscle
        and his Tom Thumb tug
can cant a combative robin till he rocks on his heels.

A deer and a killdeer have ears and can hear the feral
foot, but how is the worm warned? Unarmed,
without fang or claw, dumb as the clam, and as blind,
he not only survives, he thrives. When Darwin played music
to worms ensconced in flowerpots on the piano,

certain *low* sounds drove them underground—not
unprovided for, he found. Nor without consequence.
Worms can change landscapes! Those subterranean hordes
by their browsing move the earth, causing rocks to founder
and ruins to fall. Though they undo views, they've saved

past beauties, too, sifting salvaging dust
on the golden bowls of Ur and the Grecian urns.
Art, said the medic of Cos, is long. But life
is longer! One worm hands it on to another; and a worm
once out of the egg will fight for his life like a tiger!

*For John Heath-Stubbs*

## FLOWERFALL

One petal falls, and the whole
of the peony's globe is broken,
its garnet split open.

A dense sphere, as full
of itself as the taut, autumnal
orb of the apple,

this pent-in, close-packed flower,
shatters like a live coal and scatters
a Perseid shower.

It flickers, flashes, expires,
heaping, then lighting its pyre
with its own red fire.

Things brim with being, and fall:
the cone from the pine; the apple;
the peony, petal

by petal. Like an old star
ripe with light to the core,
they can hold no more.

The rim reached, as with wells
at the flood, the flower's cup fills,
runs over, and spills.

ROSES OF ASHES

The words are winter's:
dust unto dust! you must,
even as the rose
on an iron urn turns rust,
be raveled from form
by the worm, lose heart and head,
and have for eyes
the quenching dust instead.

But there is an eye,
more than a match for the dark,
which can see far past
our last fall into stark
and bitter dust:
that our end is not the worm,
that as iron filings
drawn by a magnet, form

roses on glass,
so out of the dark our own
cold ash will spring,
and flower on its stem of bone
again—when Truth
keeps tryst, and Love's fiery gust
breathes back the image
of man into man's dust.

# HOUSES

Like a great bronze hand holding flowers,
the earth holds up the bouquet of the houses of men,
"houses and temples and tombs" and is "not overweighted
therewith." In a south sea landscape a house with the look
of a birdcage designed by Corbusier roosts on the air.
It is "Somebody's Home in Balikh Papan," strange—

to strangers. The native, nearer, sees it as just
what it needs to be. High on its perch of poles,
and dry under thatch, it has come to terms with things
as they are where it is, and it matches Borneo's rains
and the river's rises. A sea away, somebody's
home somewhere in Sumatra stands with the stance

of stone on solid ground. Its well-groomed thatch
curves at the corners to crescents; its timbers flicker,
flecked with red lacquer and laced with mother-of-pearl.
Hibiscus and allamanda, and orchids, and the tall
banana, kept in their places, flank but are never
allowed to set foot on the path to the door, their rank

flamboyance as jealously under control as Rousseau's
jungles—made to be framed in gold. This house
attests to success won in an unruly world
where the odds are against the even more often than not,
and where bare necessity presses ahead of "success."
For those in distress, when times are worst, first things

come first—the hat before the fine feathers—
for the roofless, roofs against ruthless weather; lights
for those in the dark. Nature is canny. Consider
the creatures, how in each a wile to survive drives it
duly to shelter: a snail, assailed, to its shell,
a bug, at bay, to its dugout nearby. Beset

by winter a bee may house with a mouse; the transient
earwig hides out for hours head-down in flowers;
beetles bask beneath boards, slugs lie snug
under stones; foxes have holes, birds have nests—
but a man needs wall and roof and window and door
and bread and water and cup and candle and dish.

As to style, his domicile may be as lavish
as Aladdin's palace, or bourgeois or posh or ever
so humble; but once he crosses the sill and is in,
he's a king in the keep of his castle. That, for some,
is enough, though not for the fisherman's wife's ambitions.
Granted, her wishes grew; till the fish, who could see

no end to her greed, fled; and she, who had never,
wherever she went, strirred from the low black hut
of her discontent, ended where she began.
O for most of us, as for Thoreau, a white chateau
with a moat and swans on the Loire would just be a bore.
Some prefer to live right where they are, even in rows

of windowed boxes as like one another as igloos,
or in rooms without views in megalopolitan pueblos;
and a happy few have found their way through the woods
to an arbor on the coast of Bohemia. But wherever he is,
a man, like the cat in the adage, can look where he lists,
can roam, if he please, 'mid pleasures and palaces not his.

For sights, a city's facades are as scenic as postcards;
they picture time's changes, and the tacks and turns of taste:
an old house hiding its age behind make-believe brick;
a lapsing mansion, the white of its Greek keys peeling
and paling; or an entry set off with a lavender door
and a rare-as-emerald square of lawn; or a grille

entwined with iron ivy; or a Mondrian front
a hundred feet high whose composed and "frozen music"
of grids and glass comprises the walls of home
for some—some of the best-dressed people pass
every day through the door-manned doors. But the multitudes
who toil and spin and are not arrayed like the lilies

come and go and vanish like ants in sand
through doors which only they distinguish. Commuters
with keys, campers with compasses, know where
      they're going;
but as to the man with no plans and the meanest
means—one day's bread and one night's bed—
where the chronic drifter is going, nobody knows.

           \*     \*     \*

"Oh," cried the children, running up the raveled path,
"here's an old house that nobody lives in!" The door
was open. It was as empty within as the nut
where the worm has been, and musty; and dust lay like mold
on the boards; it was cold and still and their voices echoed
in its hollow as if in a cave; and they were afraid

and ran down the path toward home, the home that father
built—the fortress, the pharos, the sparrow's nest—
the warm and welcoming home with its comb of rooms.
Each room's a world with its own (its owner's) air,
where the clock and the bric-a-brac talk of his
        likes and lacks.
Victorian velvets and urns of ferns pleased some;

but vogues are vagrant. Some cram their rooms with *objets
d'art*, some just with *objets*. Some prefer cells.
But the intimate, twice-lit (lamp-lit and face-lit) room
like a Vuillard parlor, is still in favor; and pictures
on walls and flambeaux of flowers in vases on tables
are signs that against the malaise of monochrome life

the fight is forever. At home we're Sindbads in harbor.
At large in the world's bazaar, busy in the midst
of the buzz and bustle of business, some of being's bloom
rubs off us like silver from the faces of kings on coins.
When Clever Elsie woke from her sleep in the field,
estranged from herself by the dark, she was unsure

whether she was she. "Am I me, or someone else?
I'll go home and ask. There, they'll be sure to know."
We, too, to repair our dimmed identities, go
where we're most at home with ourselves. As for me, a turn
of the key (my "Open, Sesame!") lets me through
to a room which is unmistakably my niche

in earth's enormous nest-riddled swallow-cliff.
There on the sofa's the Issa book I was reading,
and askew on the floor that pair of unchic shoes
with the fit to my foot of the glass slipper. The day
has dazed me; but now with a wall between the noise
of the dazzle and me, I can see. I walk to the window.

As I look out, a moth looks in, both of us
light-lured—the glass an impasse for him, a pass
to the stars for me! My mind enchants me! I can match
with a glance light's lightning speed through space. I can go
anywhere "without going out of the door." With my feet
flat on the floor, I'm afloat with the Fish and the Swan—

till my own voice topples me: "Vertigo goeth before
a fall. Come down to earth. There is work to do."
Work, the two-faced, is Sisyphus' stubborn stone
and the clod that yields gold; it's the tough tiger, tamed
only by relentless love; it's the task to be grasped
like the nettle; it is dolor and ardor, serpent and dove.

A sculptor who first thought his room too scant for his scope,
fifty years later when he could create equal
in stature a towering man from an iron rib
or a matchstick man out of plaster, saw for himself
that art, which makes light of matter, can coax a camel
through a needle's eye; then he found there space and
        to spare.

In this world the self needs a cell to find itself in;
for a Navajo, it is said, a blanket will do.
For a life-battered man a room is the wayfarer's well,
the date palm's alms in the desert, the inn where the raveled
sleeve is reknit, and where we begin again
our being's business, the doing of which may move us

a notch on the way to some destined damascened brightness
that, out of this tempering fire, we may yet come to be.
A room is a loft full of straw, to be spun into gold,
and weighed. "My love is my weight," said a saint. Looking
from his latticed house one jeweled African night,
the angel of his eye led him up stairs of stars

till he stood, stunned by glory, on the sill of the City
that the One Lamp lights like a sun. And out of his House
of many mansions, God (to borrow Tiepolo's
brush), his patriarch head thrust through a rift
in forget-me-not sky, looks down on the earth-girdling houses
of men, a green galaxy garlanding time,

sees each, from Adam's "Acanthus-shaded Bower"
floored with flowers to the latest, ivyless, skyrising
tower. He hears the babel of a billion voices,
friends' and foes', and knows each man's, and each man's
mind by his own. He smells earth-odors: clover
and honeycomb, roast meats and bread made of millet
        and maize

and roots and rice, the incense of everyday life.
Good Landlord, he knows when a tenant, "Called
        home," goes
from his place. He keeps each one in his eye, and to all
who have kept the family likeness, the Father's look,
the great Householder calls, "Come!" Then out from
        the highways
and byways and all the corners and cracks of the earth

(the jealous Husbandman counts, in his thrift, every leaf
on the Vine) the kinsfolk stream toward the Father's
        House,
and find there, familiar among things made new,
        their homes,
burnished to a brightness by the buffing of life, ingrafted
in the luminous mansions; given back to their
        given-back sight;
restored, like flowers to gardens in auroral light.

# R AS IN GARNET

On a Pompeian wall a painted branch
of pomegranates conjures up brightness by the rose
on the rounded rinds, and in dim Etruscan tombs
fruit-red horses, looming, light up the leaves
of terracotta trees. The sacred red
on the crown of Ishtar's tiny image shines
from the cloud of the clay, and deep in the underworld
Persephone holds in her hand a lamp-bright fruit.

Red, like the rough weed, seeds itself everywhere,
in spring's minute vermilion spider moving
across a crimson stone, in spikelets of coral
beneath the wave, in rose-fringed shrimp on the sea-floor,
in a dove's foot, in the eye of an eel, in a shell,
in granite and garnet. It glows in the last crab leaf
that clings to the tree like an ember of summer's fire
smoldering on the umber air of autumn.
Ochre on a cold lip, on a closed eye
consigned to the clay, is a sign of hope;
bright resurrections, indeed, have already occurred,
Ra rising from death every day, and the sun's
geranium flame reappeared in the bowl and the brick,
and out of Persephone's broken fruit the flash
of a scarlet star: the seed's insistent sign
of the fiery phoenix dreaming in our clay.

## CRAYON MONSTER

Bold as Matisse with her palette of reds
and unabashed greens, as serious in play
as Klee, this earnest artist confronts you
with her crayon monster. Rampant, he rears

on seven foreboding toes like lions'
claws, and glares through narrow slits
of eyes with a look as wild as a Chinese-
opera demon's. She exaggerates

with exuberance! His rubber-balloon
face, as big as the moon, is banana-
yellow; he has arms full of monster muscles,
tigerpaw hands, and eyebrows as fierce

as thunder—enough to convince you, and yet,
the longer you look, the surer you are:
this is no honest monster. Those grass-green
curls that go round his oversize head

like a flowery lei belie him. Beneath them
he is benign. He would roar (if he roared)
"as gently as any nightingale."
He's a masquerader who only scares

to please; an age-of-innocence, children's-
hour ogre as guileless as his young
creator who views him with pride, alive
and untamed and safe in his paper cage.

## CONSIDER THE LILIES

When one of those lilies-to-be-considered was looked at,
regal in the unspun stuff of its swanwhite glory,
it seemed at a standstill in time, changeless, like a flower
of alabaster. Then, overnight, overtaken
by life's perpetual motion, the tip of a petal
turned brown—abrupt reminder that flesh is as grass,
marble as mortal as the petal, and that moment by moment
beauty's dismemberer, time (the prime mover), was moving
the elegant lily toward its inelegant end.

Like the wilting lily's, man's skin wrinkles and withers,
but the man within, like the palm by the running waters,
is renewed every day. Under inner sun he prospers
like the green bay tree. Hokusai, raptly capturing
a goldfish or hibiscus with his brush, thought ninety years
not enough! Oh, the mind, alive in its time-battered arbor
can flourish like the lily-of-the-field-in-its-prime, can cope
with cold like the winter rose that flowers in the snow,
counter dark clouds like the seven-tiered arch of the rainbow!

## SKY WRITING

Turner, watching with an artist's ardor a sunset's
floating yellows and pinks and drifts of dusky
plum as they kindled the crested clouds and turned them
slowly, from snowy gardenia to gilt goldenrod
to burning nasturtium, cried out: "The *sun* is God!"

The psalmist, gazing at the night-sky's golden graffiti:
Orion and the Lion outlined in stars; at the moon
ablaze in full bloom; or the vespertine west florescent
with fires of quince and carnelian and saffron and citron,
sang, at that cosmic candescence: "*God* is a sun!"

## INTIMATIONS OF MORTALITY

Though crowned, the Muse, each year with leafy wreath,
Mortal, she ends at last, sans hair, sans teeth.
One fallen, granite grain from Pantheon's portal
Proclaims *Ars* only *longa*, not immortal.

# SELECTED POEMS

SWAN

Some swan, serene in an expedient beauty
that molds him to the water's shifting mores
and the fluctuant airs, lies in his oval,
polished, Polynesian-boat shape, floating
light upon the lilied lake, and lifts
high his lean, enameled head set
smoothly on either side with a sober eye,
and preens a wing as fine with featherwork
as a peony with waxen petal thatch.

His all-functional fairness fits him for swan life,
in which he has need of that long, admired neck
for underwater weeding and the black bill
built for spooning seed, leaf, and spawn,
and insures that, invariably, *le cygne* becomes,
for his marble whiteness and formal, stately stance,
the center of the pastoral scene wherein
he moves with gliding elegance and snow-soft
thrust of his forward-flowering, moon-bright breast.

## THREE-TOED SLOTH

*For Patrick Boland*

In the first place, the slow sloth labors
heavily under the undue derogation
of his name, the same as the seventh deadly sin,
and secondly, somewhat suffers, in our eyes,
from the dull delusion that slowness is a defect—
though we are agreed that Rome was not built in a day.

Beethoven, to name just one, knew that the slow
is neither sinful nor sad, but just a way
of moving differently and saying something else.
The sloth is not fashioned for the gigue, he is
the molto lento movement in a fugue,
the animal andante of the suite.

Though there are those who find his stone-hinged motions
laughable, he is really no comedian;
no clown, he seriously enjoys himself,
and slowly, as some play chess. His game is with gravity,
hanging all day, opposed, resisting it,
like a clam walking broadside against a wave.

Loth to leave a present place he lingers
in it exploring its riches exhaustively,
like a bee in a rose. His movements understate
sensate felicity, as, an empiricist,
he feels his way, engaged in epicurean
loitering, in an empire of space and leaves.

His languor is fabulous; he stays so still
so long that a patina appears on him
as on unrolling stones, or domes of copper;
that mossy-stump effect or lichen-look
comes from the green mask of algae that lodge
in "certain grooves or flutings" of his hair.

To one's surprise he is always reversing himself,
and he hangs beneath branches like an inverted bird,
arrested in a perpetual state of suspense.
He sleeps with his small, round, earless, octopus
head tucked safely inward, like a pearl
in a velvet pouch, at rest on his own breast.

Unlike the birds he was never intended for walking
(having no feet) yet like them was meant for the heights;
using his claws, toucan-fashion, he climbs to the tops
of tallest trees, his back to the darkness below
and, depending there in casual, catenary sag,
resembles a last year's large, disheveled nest.

He bears himself carefully, like a child carrying
a glass of water, as if from his brimming cup
he does not want to spill one drop of enjoyment.
Energy steeps in him; he is dense with sensation
as a thinker with thought, and he hangs with closed eyes
and the concentration of someone listening to music.

TRIO IN A MIRROR

The mirror's law is clear—an eye for an eye,
its flaw, when perfect, blind conformity; it says
what it sees, but can't see deep enough, nor through a thing,
misses stars behind eyes, scars to the bone, breaking
heads, and the heart's traumas and dramas. Just a tooth
for a tooth, no more; that's the mirror's view of the truth.

Even that much-consulted mirror on the wall couldn't
tell all, though it couldn't help telling the truth; such a magic
glass, which will never connive with a wicked queen
or favor a wicked scheme, is a useful tool
in a fairy tale where the beautiful one who is good
gains all the gold and the love as we hoped she would.

It's easy if in and out coincide to see
what's there, but the in, like the beauty in Beauty's Beast,
is apt to hide. When I'm carried away by my head
I'd be shocked if I saw my unfollowing face in a glass,
for the mind is a falcon city, and thought can take flight
like the hawk from its nest and rise to a flaming height

the flesh fails to reflect (though saints with their single sight,
so illumined by what they looked at, their eyes such lamps,
could set all the night round their roof-trees alight). But I,
divided, in time coming back to myself, land
with a thud from my thought. "Can this be I?" I cry.
"My skin and bones do not reflect my joy."

No less opaque is this trio, poised to play;
here are mutable men, not Apollos, no emitters of rays,
no matter for marble; not a notable mien among them.
They show signs of life; a wrinkle, a tic, or touches
of time's tattooing, and though each has some personal quirk,
they all share the serious look of people at work.

Such is the case in the mirror; the facts are there,
evidence nothing will alter, not an ear or a nose
by a hair. Three quite ordinary men! at least
they will not attract our attention, and we've come
      not to look
but to listen. The lights go low. Across space,
      from somewhere
a single line is launched and holds on the air

like the first thread of the spider's spinning, the unforeseen
form beginning, cross-hatching and building till all is
a balance of sound. Now the liquid notes of the flute
float, serene as the water where long green willows
lean, and lilies gleam. And the fire of the cello
colors the cups of the flowers umber and yellow

as they flash, thin-blown and brittle, in the
      harpsichord's sudden
garden of glass, and tinkle and turn with the time,
fast, slow, soft, till at last, lost.
The players pause for breath—by the sweat of their brows
they are earning their bread—then again, the coughing dying,
come together and soar like a formed flock flying.

The sallies and nervous sorties of notes take shape,
composing a gilded grove where birds—Rameau's—
gather, rhythmic and rustling, in the poplars' ovals,
and settle, and sing in that sun. Then these men, attending,
like those who close their eyes for better vision
burn with the kindled concord to which they listen.

Confronted, how would they know themselves now in
        a glass—
a flawless one, free from tarnish, ripple, or scratch:
"some mistake," they would think, amazed at the false
        faces there,
unable to believe, like Eve, what they saw with their eyes
in a mere mockingbird mirror which may copy to perfection
but lacks heart and ends in an artless deception.

I am all at once aware that now I am seeing,
new, in the burning-glass of their concentration,
three heads, noble as those on Roman medals,
where the spirit glows in the bone and the two are joined—
unlovely shapes made lovely by love's katharsis—
in the crystal of music. I, too, with the trio discern this.

The ear is craned. Such intentness is tinder. By the spark
struck off I am looking, past that glass face I can see
any time, at a profile that gleams in the dark as if pencilled
in silver. It excites. It is sibyl, like a sculptured angel,
all felicity augured in the limestone eyes. Thus set free,
I am no longer my cloud; I can see light through me.

No matter to the artist if his face hides his light like
    a bushel,
he can set his candlestick high and shine through his art.
He can say, "Never mind my looks; mind my music, marbles,
and pictures; the best of me, after all, is in my books."
But in meetings head-on, it's the face one sees, the
    coin's obverse
that counts, though the brightness of Adonis may adorn
    the reverse.

My eyes turn outward, meant for other things;
I cannot see myself as others do.
My news is secondhand; I count on echoes
and cold reflections to give me back a picture of myself
to look at. Eye to eye, detached as an island on a map,
I contemplate my image imprisoned in the shining trap.

Now my mirror becomes my clock and cautions me,
daily: tick, tock, no bolt or lock
can keep time from carrying you away;
see, one hair's gone and others going, grey;
the lines are longer. It tells me straight in the eye,
with delphic sang-froid, "one of these days you will die."

Once meant for the rich and fair, mirrors were rare,
what's left of them rarer still: old shells of gold,
a T'ang bronze, its dragon gone green with the years,
dim disks of tin, or that curious thing from Peru—
of pyrites, polished and patched like a terrapin's carapace;
it would make a cubist puzzle of anyone's face.

But the urge to see for oneself is everywhere;
ladies have always looked: Lais and Venus;
Penelope, probably; Helen, and little Nell as well;
even Punch's Judy hunting for a small patch of beauty;
and water is good matter for reflection if one lacks glass
as the shepherd saw, with his sheep by the pool in the grass,

and the goosegirl gazing in the moonlit well, and notorious
Narcissus, fairly caught in his own spell.
Dazed by this dazzle, I'm lost in a labyrinth of mirrors,
misled by reflections. Though I'm not afraid, in an age
when a mouse may be found in a maze but no
        minotaur's about,
I'm sadly in need of a thread. Is there no way out?

Logical Alice first looked, next walked straight
        through the glass,
at once proceeded to see what she'd come for, and then,
satisfied not to stay, returned, in the same direct way.
Without questions a mirror's a dead end, and always
        turns us
back face to face with ourselves. To resolve our doubt
logic of some sort is needed; let's *ask* our way out

of the glare of these blinding alleys. Where in the world
do we think we are going and what does this looking lead to?
To know we'd need to go back to Adam in Eden
and that primal trouble with the apple; we can
        hardly say, now,
who we are, or what for, in this altered case of our calling;
since that most original fall, we are always falling.

Broken, mended, shaky, patched-up creatures
with cracks in our minds, we often lose sight of ourselves;
we look, as St. James said, and go away, and forget,
and come back to look again at that icon there in full color
on the glass page; we consult it as we would a lexicon
to be sure of a word when memory can't be depended on.

(The mirrors angels are, are deep, are meres
drawing all they can hold of light from the one Sun
trillions exhaust no more than a single one.
Their shining, like thought, gathers stature, towers in a wave,
till they blaze in total bliss, and their turning toward us
drenches our roused souls in those luminous torrents.)

What draws us back to this magnet of silvery blankness
("There is none so homely but loves a looking-glass.")
pitting hope ("things *do* change!") against fact. Is it blunt
          wit,
vain as the caught carp's bumping against the pane?
or is there some sign, ant-egg or mustard-seed size,
hatching but not yet surfaced, not ripe yet for eyes?

Tell us, mirror on our wall, how we happen to seek
in a crowd of reflections and shadows, past sight, for
          something,
ideal or dream, we've never seen? Why is it
we find the ugly unfair, not at all what the flesh
was meant to be heir to, and as for beauty, assume
a family right, as to an unforgettable heirloom?

"The hunger we're born with pushes us, each to his pasture,
the worm to the walnut, the eye into orchards of light.
'Ignoti nulla cupido,' says Ovid: no hunger
for what you don't know; and you know you want more than
    I show—
unless you see through me; for here are only the skins
of things, and the buds; here beauty only begins."

What a roundabout way to discover all's not in the picture,
that the mirrored face, like a buffeted rose losing
its battle with beetles, has not realized what it's meant for.
Happy fault, the flaw, which offending, lets us see we have eyes
for the perfect, for the end of becoming, the last, not the first;
it's the golden apple of matter for which we thirst.

Is there a glass like the King's daughter's, never misled?
Not one! though music, for a moment, may mirror a man
to the heart of his heart, or heads so blaze with life
that the light thrusts through, as in crystals, till the bones
        utter it.
"You are gods!" God said. But you are dark. A cloud is
    on the star,
and not a mirror in the world can show how beautiful you are.

# AFTERNOON OF A GNAT

Stranger to time and the obsolete egg, estranged
from the maggot past and never minding a mother,
the gnat, at once full size and fully wise—
like skull-born Minerva—springs from the bursting shell

and joins the cloud, at home in the social whirl
where, heir to a gap, he adds his diamond-chip shape
and dizzy step to the dionysiac dance
crazing the midday glaze with a maze of z's.

Still in his sphere at dusk floating in violet,
his wheel still wound, he rides his singular cycle
in the time allowed, till quick as he came he comes
to a natural end for a gnat—in a swift swallow.

A CONCERN FOR BEAUTY

Who will cavil at a concern for beauty
such as the placing of this potted gorgon's head
with the green stiletto leaves or eel-grass
electrified in all directions in the window
of a modest establishment, a barber shop?
One would not wish to condemn a flair (though faint)
for form, as shown in this elemental attempt
at symmetry: space with an object in its middle.

Here is the bristling outline of an extrovert
with nothing supine about it like hair on the head;
it looks like a vegetable hedgehog; if it were animal
one would say that it appeared frightening because frightened.
It is not, precisely, a prepossessing plant
but it provokes speculation and invites comparisons
like the dark lady of the sonnets, or the sphinx,
or other poetic presences that haunt our air.

It is a kind of mathematico-symbolic head
with thoughts projecting sword-like from every point;
it is sunburst, spiny sphere, gem with congealed rays,
a fountain's caricature, an isometric
explosion, or the abstract image of an acrid
and echinate personality, definitely
a desert type imitable in such media
as plastic, glass, or stiffly wired horsehair.

One may feel he is looking on beauty a little bare
viewing through glass this unaccompanied shrub.
But who dreams of asking more of a sky than one sun?
A monomial organization at least eliminates
redundancy; and for those who care for such things
there is precedent: Wordsworth's single violet
by a stone, and the calm of an uncrowded canvas with
one hill or one heron, enough for a Japanese eye.

Sometimes an excess of space is necessary to a scene,
like long idle lawns leading to a ruin
or expanses of velvet as foil for one emerald's fire.
This plant armed heavily with spines needs space
like a ballerina who must have room for the circle
of her skirts, like a swan in need of an empty oval,
a background sky, a cloud, a mirror, or a river
for the adequate rendition of its classic profile.

Here in a magic-lantern scene is centered a green sun,
a glittering planet that glows through gilt air toward the eye
like an aquarium-denizen outspread in its tentacle-wreath,
gleaming through glass like a watermark through paper.
Its maker has entered imagination's secret groves
and achieved, along with the shapers of fountains, arches,
and facades, a personal transmutation of space,
enlarging the landscape of the world with one bright island.

CHINESE BABY ASLEEP

She has the immaculate look of the new,
like the bud of the rose just showing through
its shell of separating sepals.

That seal with the sheen of silk, her skin,
encircles a seedling sun within
as rinds go round the stars in apples.

Eyelid and lip are luminous, lit
by the glow of life, by her breath as it
flows in and out like light through opals.

*For Walter*

## SPIDER COMPARED TO STAR

If one considers attentively the radiant spider
(momentarily moved behind a purple cumulus of aster
but emerging now, the legs outspread in rays,
eight spokes curved from a center scintillant like an asterisk
spaced on pale paper) one sees her starwise.

Head and elliptic maw are in close conjunction
like the merging orbs of a double star; like Rigel
she has no neck: S after all is for swans not stars
which are involute and dispense with antennae,
        horns, and tails,
retaining (with spiders) only a wreath of retractile rays
whereby the air twinkles set in motion around them.
She is Venus with diamond eyes that gleam like a cat's,
set four-square like the four perfect four-pointed
stars of gold in a floret the size of a fly.
She possesses, waiting for prey, the patience of the fishermen
fiery above in their boats of "millions of years."
(A billion to one is a rough relation of time,
and a spider's night-watch would equal three million years
of star-life.) She is silent, too, as they,
as still as the stony light of an extinct star
that comes to us late like the flower of the dinosaur's footprint

or the spiral bouquet of an ammonite's filigree sutures
since Mesozoic days preserved impeccable under sea-glass.

In June a golden garden-spider floating
slowly across a sky of irises,
neither aimless nor idle, her net nailed
to rafters of roses, shakes with her foot
the diamond outline specked with a black and gold
      enamel of gnats,
impassive moves in the midst of a meteor-shower of bees
and comet-wasps stinging the air with fiery whips.
In autumn when dahlias light their ruby lamps
and the gilt grape-leaf hangs, worn to a web by
      waves of weather,
the spiders stir among the yellow zinnias
and tall chrysanthemums, cinnamon-colored and curved
petal by petal inwardly to solid globes,
moving from point to point in their orbits, sure-footed
      over chasms
like the high stars across invisible bridges.

An aerial firmament stretches above the grass a foot or two
like a reduction through glass of airy oceans above.
There suns and mimic constellations stand,
Aldebaran looming large in his silver isosceles
and clear Canopus caught in a skein of light.
Milky ways of web shine across meadows,
and galaxies hang with their islands of black over gardens,
and many unpredictable moons appear,
lemon-yellow or white with shadows of lilac,
and turn on their spiral paths tenacious as planets.
("Geometry, that is to say, the science
of harmony in space, presides over everything.")
In the silence one hears the eloquent spiders and the stars
speak with the incontrovertible voices of things,
saying that certainly the deducible precedes the deduction
and things necessarily antedate theories; they say that
matter is music and sings with iridescent voice
like water moving polychromatic from stone to stone.
Recurring themes built on the tones of a primitive scale
appear now here, now there, in rich confusion,
islands of blue above in the Milky river,
and a white Bear walking the polar sky; below,
echo of skies in the grass, the dew-drop blur
of the Pleiades, and a tarantula rayed
like golden Algol fierce among the minor stars.

# CHARM

Echoes of Orpheus' magic lyre still linger
in the wreath of the animal ear like the singing sea
in acoustic spires of shell: one sees how the cobra
obeying the flute flows from his flattened coil
upward and flowers upon a vertical stem,
and one hears—what an Irish idea!—that the snail has an ear
for music, that kismet is come for the mollusk for whom
the coloratura blackbird's bell-song peals!

Whether a fact or a fiction one pictures the action,
the thrush's sudden serenading glissando
sounding some latent *attrait* in the listening snail
who glides from his grapeleaf tent on a ruffled foot
in rhythmic ripplings, and stops, procured,
the flattered Muse of this music-for-an-occasion
whose bravura, cadenza, and trills are all for him
as the opulent iridescences of the web
are all for the fly; moveless and mesmerized
he waits beside his white Ionic wheel
in an anesthesia of dreams, trapped in his now
enchanted need to know the end of the song.

## CARDINAL'S CHICK

He has discovered the world. Slipped
from the hedge, like a child through an unlatched door,
the adventurer stands, tousled, bland,
with a soft lamb-look, an awkward and avid
novice still in that auric age
when nectar and aphids freely fall
to his lot. He has the charm of the baby
ibex of oölite found in the cave,
the same ingénue eye. He's an icon
of innocence: thistledown-breasted, fawn-
fuzzed, infant-crested, flat
on his long, pronged feet in a minimal puddle.

# POSTCARD: BONES OF A SABRE-TOOTHED TIGER

Is this a tiger that I see before me?
this gaunt, bald, Brobdingnagian ruin?
Such a riddled sphinx is a riddling theme for a card
of greeting! What is its meaning? A winter's tale
with the acrid moral that we are ashes, merely,
and mortal? No, clearly, bones that rise and stand
on their feet like the phoenix merit a fairer reading,
not memento mori, but memoranda

of life, lived as if loved. Though that stony form
has the stopped look of things with the current cut off—
vine leaves in a vase or a foot in phenol—see
the unquenchable verve, the nervous stance of the cat
stalking some mammoth eocene rat, smoothly,
scarcely turning a hair of the ten-foot ferns.
What engineering finesse this hunter had!
But carnivorous time has devoured the tiger, too,

to the bones, picked by scientists, polished and prized
as ivories, pieced, part by part to a whole, with the bliss
of a papyrologist matching his papery flakes,
and as knowledgeably, so that if the monster should fall,
all the resources of all the key men can quickly
put him together again. Itemized, from the tip
of his tail to the terrible tooth and the toes that turn up
in rosettes, they have summed him up in numbers, and yet,

though numbers count, they can't account for him
to the three little boys with arithmetic books in their hands
and their heads full of wonders and Grimm imagination.
When they look at the giant of bone that towers above them
the jungle comes creeping back and the tiger takes on
his bristling breastplate of fur and glistening sabre;
a vulcan rumble roars through the corridors
and a green eye glares again in the cavernous socket!

## SERENADE

The tin-type tune the locusts make,
Scarlatti-like, among the green
enameled grasses, plucking lutes
of parchment wing with plectrum leg,
ticks off in tones itinerant lives,
and tells in tryst-inviting trills
how love, in miniature modes
and minor forms, perpetuates
the constant, shapely themes of things,
and on melodic clocks records
a transient, true, and treasured bliss.

## ALEXANDRINA

Alexandrina has shy eyes. Her name recalls
palaces, chariots, Persian horses, classical
glories now gone, like butterflies from autumn air.
Alexander of Macedon wanted the world, and everywhere
detained his dream with deeds so that echoes of empires
won by him for a little while, and lost forever,
still stir. The great reverberations of his fame
sound down the balustrades of time his royal name
like thunder, little by little diminishing till dim
and distant. Alexandrina has never heard of him.

What power is in a name? is it a magical transfer
of fame or virtue like eating the heart of the tiger?
or a pretty charm, like a gift of flowers, to take one away
from the tedious, the mean and unglamorous everyday?
Dawns have colored the Doric-columned porticoes
of oracles, and now on warped doorways of the Rose
and Royal cafes, with peeled and blue façades, the sun
rises, and lights, like votive candles offered to Fortune,
faded letters that spell out these dream-projected names
asserting in pseudo-sibyl style impossible claims.

Through the everyday grey there glitters a sprinkle of
    diamond dust;
crowns and haloes persist on the air like leaves of acanthus
shapely among the marble fragments; Sir Galahad
hangs on the schoolroom wall, and the name of Helen, now flat
and faint as a pressed flower, is heard in the halls. Broken
profiles of nobler views linger, visible or spoken,
in a penny print, a rhyme, a coin, or a quotation.
Desire moves by an irreducible attraction
in moth-flights around the ideal whose tokens adhere in the world
like flakes of gilt on time-darkened figures once all gold.

Alexander acquired under his sky, lavish with constellations,
kingdoms and golden things of men's imaginations,
and above the muddy horizon must rise some one faint star
whereby the world of things is widened for Alexandrina,
adding a china fawn to the painted pots of ivy
and a plastic diadem for her lapel on Sunday.
Alexander's armor, his helmet's silver leaf-scroll, shining,
and Alexandrina's flowered apron and bargain stocking
are but circumstantial evidence and cannot impart
information regarding riches palaced, possibly, in a heart.

*For Sandy Conheim*

## SNOWFLAKES

New come, complete, with no precursive bud,
stemless as stars, a migrant multitude
like the white bloom of orchards blown abroad,
snowflakes in floating millions slowly crowd,
each adding the small medallion of its face
to the tall mosaic flowering on space.

Sprouted from water, in winter, and spurred by the cold,
these spangled figures come and go; though they glow
from manifold facets, like carbons, their sparkling flesh,
shaped on an adamant law, will break at a breath;
crystals too tender, conditioned to air, to be held
between finger and thumb, they melt from sight when felt.

Not by arduous art, as marble makes roses of walls
in the Taj Mahal, but by nature this mineral falls,
always, in intricate flakes whose isinglass grounds,
spiked and eyeleted, angled and rayed all round,
unfailingly form to fairness on a root of six
like the comb's hexagonal honey-urns of wax.

Arrayed on glittering ribs, star within star
within star within star, extending their fabric as far
as these crystals can, held to the scope of a scheme,
they reach by finished means their finest extreme,
distilled to filigranes of snow as ornate
as the florets that silver a surface of Persian brocade.

## FOR PETER WHO CRIED
## BECAUSE HE COULD NOT CATCH THE MOTH

Peter, this epode of tears that follows chagrin
is classic form for the human state you are in,
as, distinctly stung by the insect's instinctive evasion,
you display the normal (for your age) response to frustration.

The moth does not cry for the moon, but struck by the light
pursues it headlong in fascinated flight,
and lacking the requisite mental reactions for tears
beats its breast and profitlessly perseveres.

The power to choose is more choice than the prize, and you
chasing the moth in his path want what you do,
while he, determined creature, willy nilly
circles the globe of a barren electric-lily.

Child, this fly-by-night is a shy, wild thing
with an easily crumpled paper-thin gold-tissue wing
not fit for caressing. (*Can* you coldly understand,
at three, that a moth in the air is worth two in the hand?)

An Aladdin's lamp (and you have one) will when you will
bring him enchanted to stand on an azure sill
with his ruffled and sulphur silks before and behind
lit up full-view by the Argus-eyed moon of your mind.

## WHEELS

Wheels are works of wit: the Greek with their neat
corollas, four-petaled and formed of metal and air;
the barrow's Cyclops eye, and the spider-web circles
that twinkle on cycles, and the airy rings on gigs,
all spare compared to the Japanese coach's twin giants:
full-flowered, thirty-spoked, yellow chrysanthemum wreaths.

The early world got the wheel and it was as welcome
as camels to nomads, a comfort in this vale of friction
where it takes things lightly; a prime mover like seven
league boots, it's an ornament, too, gliding with the calm
of a swami unmindful of time or place, everywhere
with an equal grace; suavely; the swan of the streets.

It carried kings to and fro in Sumeria, Naxos,
Assyria; it was the star of the chariot era
flashing through fields with satellite lions to war;
it rolled the carts on the cobbles, the prams in the parks,
and bowled down boulevards smoothing the path for elegant
Manet ladies poised in their polished calash.

Dappling the air with a firework flaring and falling,
the wheel performs like sun on petals of glass
in a rose window, like wind exposing the silver
concealed under leaves; wheels do what fountains do
to light, pick it apart and cast it aside,
diverted, divided, and brilliantly multiplied.

Even when old and abandoned in battle or barnyards,
propped against fences, battered and scarred, they still sparkle
like the gold-leaved wreath when the victor's head has fallen;
their irrepressible rays—signals that say
we lose our vision unless we look—make all
our vertical values, so prone to collapse, stand up.

The wheel, beginning to move, moves *us* in its whirl;
we are carried away by the radiant change in the facts
as the axle turns up gold in the ore of the air
and a cloud of dust is churned to blue mosaic,
and commerce becomes a concourse of planets, distant
cousin to the floating traffic of uncrowded stars.

## WILD PLUMS AT PHA-AN

Here is a twilight-piece; in the muted scene
The lake lies pearl beneath the opaline
Shell of sky, and spaces of amethyst light
Open wide like flowers, on the edge of night,
And a pale, towery, dimmed-by-distance hill
Rests on the silver water, shadowier still.

Pink sifts through the nebulous plum-tree mist
Of flowers floating lightly in swanshaped drifts,
And out of paling sky nacreous shadows pass
Across a damask of leafage still as glass;
The lessening light, mute as a moving moth,
Mottles with lambent mauves the plum-flower cloth.

On the left a crescent cart of basketry, curved
Like the satin scoop in the fruit where the seed is stored,
Has stopped. The two wheels, quiet as unwound clocks,
Are ritual circles behind the chalk-white ox
Standing impassive with hieratic mask
And animal eyes that neither seek nor ask.

The driver sits, motionless, like a small
Ivory carving, in a closely folded shawl,
Crouched, with the patience of a plant upon its root,
And secret with the simple secrecy of fruit.
But the one who reclines in the curve of the cart has come
To transfer the transformation of the plum

In the late light, recomposed on a mirror-eye
That takes lake, light, and violet sky
Within, into a magical solitude
Where the swan-winged trees may be forever viewed
In a landscape turned to a pure Arcadian kind
Enhanced by the fadeless gilding of the mind.

## PERENNIAL LANDSCAPE

In the manner of water winding over stone
ambient time moves among marble leaves
in attenuating autumns, or laps upon
some gilded Buddha's granite lip erasing
by gradual grains its glyptic contour, for,
ever since the insinuate serpent flowed down the tree,
full of wiles and a will to make nothing of man's world,
and filed with the silken rasp of his tongue the hinge
of Paradise, time, turned to undoing,
pipes with a chronic, disenchanting wail
that draws matter in slow retreat from form;
so towers topple and stone hair slowly falls.

But a single eyebrow left intact on the limestone
attests now to the past presence of passion,
and one now-delighted eye to passion present still,
for counter to time there runs the perennial current
of a purely personal temper and taste for love,
and as from the deathless pith of Paradise
flowers in time re-rise, as surely in Paris or Venice
somebody's Venus smiles, or dark sphinx frowns
from fresher stone, and time fails, foiled
by lovers whose ceaseless sequences of visions
committed to ivory, oak, or rock, revise
with unravaged profiles the landscape's successive abrasions.

*For Steve and Shirley*

## SKYBLUE MONDAY

It was one of those days that dazzle; we looked at the world
through the rosy lunettes of the weather and walked on
        clouds
across a scintillant river to an isle with a Sindbad-
diamond-valley glitter where the blades of grass
shone as if sheathed in glass, and the million miles
of sky within view were an absolute lazuline blue.

We went down a willow-blurred path toward a pure
        white peony
patch which, as we approached it, softly exploded
and floated away in swans. From behind a tree
that habitué of Persian gardens, the peacock,
sauntered, his sapphire-pansy petaled breast
stippled with gold at every step, while above

on a stem, fluffed-out like a flower of fur, sat a tiny
monkey the color of ginger. We watched while a child
with parrot-red socks stopped by the cassowary's cage,
and ignoring the extraordinary stranger there
said, "oh" at an almost invisible sparrow. And then,
having left the lion to his den and the condor asleep

in a corner, we browsed indoors with the pampered orchids,
all opals and frills, where a trickle of water tumbled
with a toy-size sound down stones and on and around
the calico-patterned jade the mosses made,
and saw the banana tree under the bell and how
it held at its side its yellow umbrella of fruit.

The day, like being in love, seemed reason—for being—
enough; and at sunset the pink-scaled river shimmered,
inlaid like a mask from Malaya with mother-of-pearl;
above us was Venus in a sea of roses, and tinted
like ribbons of rainbows, people went drifting past
        fountains
and willows, under gilded skies and garlands of gulls.

*For Jerry and Linda*

## GIRANDOLE

In the dark at first, we see things in their sleep
like seeds locked up in pods, cocoons, and burs,
each with its sphinx's face persuading us:
"Our looks are black, but we're really beauties. Wait
and see." And we do, till one day some dove of a dawn
comes in on a pink wing, singing, "Wake up!"

Then there's a stir—an unfolding, unfurling, undoing
of knots, shaking off of shells as infants outgrow
their eggs; the roe spills over in silver, and out
of each buried bean a green head butts itself free;
and the rose goes, or the snail, on its way, unrolling
its roundest corolla. Oh, the view opens up to our eye!

And see what baroque embellishments ensue
as throngs of things take shape and place in space:
the fantail vine hung with the golden horde
of its hundred gourds; and bright in its broken shell
a pomegranate's swarm of garnets; moonshine,
pine-tree waves, and skies all mackerel scallops.

Once a fortunate friction ignites the fuse—presto!
chrysalids burst into blue, the firework flowers
go up in sparks, the fountain towers—and the story's told.
Breaking through clouds the sun leaps forth and we see
for ourselves: the black bird's gold and the world—
    what a sight!—
is a girandole, a ring of things—all lights.

# PEOPLE

People are destinations in our adventure,
are lands and landscapes, cities, islands, worlds,
each, with its unknown prospects and perspectives,
waiting, like Beauty behind the umbrageous hedge,
discovery and delight's delineation,
fame and a name in the map of someone's heart.

Arcadia! where is it? happy land,
unmapped, unpromised, known as fair, and looked for
everywhere? Is it far? Shall we ever find it?
We can only follow the gothic rumor that rises,
slender, on every air, and keep to the path
that the stars pick out. Columbus, heading west,

unmoved by mountains, calm when becalmed, met
in the end more than a match for his wish, and gained
what the bartered jewels had never bargained for;
and the undomestic Polos, enamored of marvels,
outfaced faceless phantoms and parted the winds
to find a dreamed-of Flower. But these are epic

odysseys. Over local beaches, too,
the skies are blue and the moon comes out, so for those
who haven't the time or the dream, whose wagons
      are hitched,
though not to stars, there are shorter trips, to Hesperides
nearer home, where dragons are scaled to size
and the trees, well-trimmed, bear gold-plated fruit,
      within reach.

On a day undivined from the rest, a lucky turn
in the right direction and one may arrive at once,
go round a bend and see upon a lawn
a perfect little ivory city stand,
with windows lit and WELCOME on the mat,
and claim this inland island for one's own.

But embarkations begin anywhere every day
by camel, cabin cruiser, cab, or tram,
or train or plane or foot or elevator,
and the narrowest window opens on some kind of view—
a rose in a pot, a pond, or the diamond Dipper—
it's a man's inner ambit determines which one he will see.

Some, wherever they are, find out the exotic,
scenting on neighborhood air a fragrant shore
where Sinamon groweth and Pearle, and locate close at hand
an Arabia Felix, reached by a gold oak stair.
Others, the local type, not at home abroad,
may wander for years and never leave home behind.

The traveler goes, though often not as he pleases;
weather detains, detours, dissuades, deludes him;
mirage and blunder take him out of his way.
He may drift for days, or miss the boat, or get off
the bus too soon and find himself, too late,
a lotus-fancier lost among aspidistras.

Blow! oh, blow us, uncontrary wind,
somewhere where something shines; show us
a faceted city, all topaz, set in a sunset,
or a peak, a unique one like Fujiyama with high dawn
gilding its lily, sights to record in our journal!
But these are too few and far away for Monday

and Tuesday life, and others, that sparkle and catch
our eye, for all their glitter are not our goal—
how often the traveler finds to his chagrin
a handsome facade and nothing of interest within.
And if we do glimpse, once or twice, the real and the rare,
where enchantments of distance stay on in the close-up view,

and the beautiful is also the true—as we see it
in old stone palaces, frescoed on water, and amber
and floating in light—alas, their inner splendors
are closed to the public, are inaccessible
to tourists gliding past in a gondola's shell
as Lhasa's doors or the domed egg of the roc.

We learn to evade, when we can, the protean climate
where polar cold and darkening violets shift
without warning to sun and summer, and back again,
preferring an equilibrium such as one finds
in a Sung scene with a profiled pine and a waterfall
balanced by mist which keeps its golden distance.

And we do, here and there, discover compatible coasts
that welcome us, ones that we like to come back to,
whose climates and clouds are ours, and groves agree,
and planets fit our fancy's horoscope.
Happy the day when our course, like a well-starred sky,
shows names, to us famous and dear, on the maps of our love!

Happy when we can count on familiar shores
an ideal city or two, the unhideable kind
that for all its conforming contours and modest walls
and law and order within cannot contain
the music it makes, its lights, its praise—the rays
break forth anyway, and shine toward us from its hill.

But the near is the dearer view, the one after all
we've decided to live with, familiarity breeding
content, the eye at home among inhabiting
beauties, the collector-heart there where its treasure
of pictures is, greeting the everyday scene
with the untarnished welcome we feel for the sun
        and the moon.

A lover's inventory is never ended;
when we know every bank where the wild thyme blows,
        and no stone
has been left unturned, and the lilies and quinces are listed—
then something new shows up, like Brahe's star when it broke
from the dark like a chick out of its shell—and the last
is first in our eyes, and we start all over again.

Our universe expands like a garden growing
daily in flowers; how shall we ever find time
to discover it all? Oh, we've only to *start* in time—
we can go on looking forever and never a landscape's
immortal face escape us or light fade
from these nightless worlds, They are worlds
        without end. Amen.

*Kudzu* is the penultimate production of the Pourboire Press, founded by Peter Kaplan in 1974 and directed by him until his death in 1977. The book was designed by Keith Waldrop, with typesetting by Suzanne Hill. Printed by the William R. Brown Company in an edition of 500 copies, of which 50 are bound in cloth.

The portrait of the author was drawn by Jacqueline Donnelly.